Parenting 101: Practical Strategies for Raising a Happy and Healthy Child

Barley Nicola

Published by Barley Nicola, 2024.

While every precaution has been taken in the preparation of this book, the publisher assumes no responsibility for errors or omissions, or for damages resulting from the use of the information contained herein.

PARENTING 101: PRACTICAL STRATEGIES FOR RAISING A HAPPY AND HEALTHY CHILD

First edition. April 2, 2024.

Copyright © 2024 Barley Nicola.

ISBN: 979-8224017027

Written by Barley Nicola.

Table of Contents

Chapter 1: Introduction 1

Chapter 2: Building a Strong Parent-Child Bond 5

Chapter 3: Setting Boundaries and Discipline 9

Chapter 4: Promoting Healthy Habits.. 13

Chapter 5: Fostering Emotional Intelligence................................. 17

Chapter 6: Supporting Academic Success 21

Chapter 7: Encouraging Independence 25

Chapter 8: Strengthening Family Relationships 28

Chapter 9: Managing Screen Time and Technology 32

Chapter 10: Handling Challenging Behaviors 35

Chapter 11: Nurturing Creativity and Imagination...................... 39

Chapter 12: Dealing with Special Needs and Differences.............. 43

Chapter 13: Cultivating Gratitude and Positivity 47

Chapter 14: Connecting with Other Parents 50

Chapter 15: Balancing Work and Family Life................................ 54

Chapter 16: Navigating Transitions and Milestones..................... 58

Chapter 17: Conclusion.. 62

Chapter 1: Introduction

- The importance of effective parenting

Effective parenting is crucial for the overall well-being and development of a child. It not only shapes a child's behavior and personality but also plays a significant role in their emotional and social growth. Parents are the primary caregivers and role models for their children, and the way they interact with them has a lasting impact on their lives. Research has shown that children who have involved and supportive parents are more likely to succeed academically, have healthier relationships, and exhibit positive behavior.

One of the key aspects of effective parenting is creating a nurturing and supportive environment for the child. This involves providing love, care, and attention to the child, as well as setting boundaries and expectations. Parents need to strike a balance between being warm and affectionate and being firm and consistent in their discipline. Children thrive in environments where they feel safe, loved, and valued, and it is the role of parents to create this type of atmosphere for their children.

Effective parenting also involves being actively involved in a child's life and taking an interest in their activities and interests. This means spending quality time with the child, engaging in activities together, and showing genuine interest in their thoughts and feelings. By being present and engaged in their child's life, parents can build a strong bond with them and create a sense of security and trust. This, in turn, helps children develop a positive self-image and fosters a sense of confidence and self-esteem.

Communication is another essential aspect of effective parenting. Parents need to communicate openly and honestly with their children, listen to their concerns and emotions, and provide guidance and support when needed. Effective communication helps children feel heard and understood and strengthens the parent-child relationship. It is important for parents to create a safe and open environment where children feel comfortable expressing themselves and talking about their thoughts and feelings.

Setting boundaries and enforcing rules is also crucial for effective parenting. Children need structure and consistency in their lives, and parents play a vital role in setting boundaries and providing guidance and discipline. By setting clear expectations and consequences for behavior, parents help children learn right from wrong and develop a sense of responsibility and accountability. Consistent discipline also helps children understand the importance of following rules and respecting authority, which are essential skills for success in life.

In addition to creating a nurturing and supportive environment, being actively involved in a child's life, communicating effectively, and setting boundaries, effective parenting also involves being a positive role model for the child. Children learn by example, and parents need to demonstrate positive behavior, values, and attitudes in their own lives. By modeling kindness, respect, honesty, and integrity, parents can teach their children important life lessons and help them develop into compassionate, responsible, and well-adjusted individuals. Parents play a critical role in shaping their child's behavior, personality, and future success. By creating a nurturing and supportive environment, being actively involved in their child's life, communicating effectively, setting boundaries and rules, and being positive role models, parents can help their children thrive and reach their full potential. It is important for parents to remember that parenting is a continuous learning process, and that by being loving, involved, and supportive, they can make a lasting impact on their children's lives.

- Overview of key parenting strategies

Parenting is a complex and multifaceted task that involves nurturing, guiding, and supporting children as they grow and develop. There are many different approaches to parenting, each with its own set of principles and strategies. In this overview, we will discuss some key parenting strategies that have been shown to be effective in promoting healthy child development and fostering positive parent-child relationships.

One important parenting strategy is to establish and maintain a strong bond with your child. Research has consistently shown that children who have secure attachments to their caregivers are more likely to thrive emotionally, socially, and academically. Building a strong relationship with your child involves spending quality time together, listening to their thoughts and feelings, and providing emotional support and guidance. It also includes setting clear boundaries and expectations, while also showing empathy and understanding towards your child's needs and emotions.

Another key parenting strategy is to use positive discipline techniques that focus on teaching and guiding children rather than punishing them. Positive discipline involves setting clear and consistent rules and consequences, while also using positive reinforcement and praise to encourage good behavior. This approach helps children develop self-control, problem-solving skills, and empathy towards others. It also fosters a sense of respect and trust between parent and child, which is essential for building a healthy and supportive relationship.

Effective communication is also a crucial component of successful parenting. Parents who communicate openly and honestly with their children are better able to understand their needs and concerns, and to provide the support and guidance they need. Effective communication involves active listening, empathy, validation of feelings, and clear, respectful communication of expectations and boundaries. By fostering open and honest communication with your child, you can strengthen your relationship and build a foundation of trust and support that will benefit both of you in the long run.

Consistency is another key parenting strategy that is essential for promoting positive child development. Children thrive on routines and predictability, so it's important for parents to establish consistent rules, routines, and expectations. Consistency helps children feel safe and secure, develop self-discipline, and understand the consequences of their actions. It also helps parents create a sense of order and structure in the home, which can reduce stress and conflict for both parent and child. By being consistent in your parenting approach, you can help your child develop a sense of security and stability that will support their growth and development.

To recapitulate, self-care is an often overlooked but essential parenting strategy. Parenting can be a demanding and stressful job, and it's important for parents to take care of themselves in order to effectively care for their children. Self-care involves taking time for yourself to rest, relax, and recharge, as well as seeking support from friends, family, or a therapist when needed. By prioritizing your own well-being and mental health, you can become a better, more patient, and more effective parent for your child. By implementing key parenting strategies such as building a strong relationship with your child, using positive discipline techniques, fostering effective communication, maintaining consistency, and practicing self-care, you can support your child's healthy development and create a positive and nurturing environment for them to thrive. Remember that no parent is perfect, and it's okay to seek help and support when needed. By approaching parenting with an open heart and mind, you can cultivate a loving and supportive relationship with your child that will last a lifetime.

Chapter 2: Building a Strong Parent-Child Bond

- Creating a loving and nurturing environment

Creating a loving and nurturing environment is essential for the well-being and development of individuals, whether they are children, teenagers, or adults. A loving and nurturing environment is one where individuals feel supported, valued, and cared for, leading to positive outcomes in terms of emotional and mental health, as well as overall happiness and fulfillment. In such an environment, individuals are encouraged to express themselves, take risks, and grow, knowing that they will be met with understanding and compassion.

One of the key elements of creating a loving and nurturing environment is the presence of strong and positive relationships. These relationships can be between family members, friends, colleagues, or even with oneself. When individuals have healthy and supportive relationships in their lives, they are more likely to feel secure and confident, which in turn can lead to increased resilience in the face of challenges and setbacks. It is important for individuals to have people in their lives who they can turn to for support, guidance, and encouragement, as well as for celebration and joy.

Another important aspect of creating a loving and nurturing environment is the ability to communicate effectively and empathetically. Communication is key to building and maintaining healthy relationships, as it allows individuals to express their thoughts, feelings, and needs in a clear and respectful manner. When individuals feel heard and understood, they are more likely to feel connected and valued, which can help to foster a sense of belonging and acceptance. It is important for individuals to listen actively and attentively to others, and to show empathy and understanding in their interactions, in order to create a safe and supportive space for communication to flourish.

In addition to strong relationships and effective communication, creating a loving and nurturing environment also involves setting clear boundaries and expectations. Boundaries are important for maintaining a sense of safety and security, as they help to define what is and is not acceptable in terms of behavior and treatment. Setting boundaries can also help individuals to prioritize their own well-being and needs, and to assert themselves in a healthy and assertive way when necessary. It is important for individuals to establish boundaries that are respectful and reasonable, and to communicate them clearly and consistently to others.

Furthermore, creating a loving and nurturing environment involves fostering a sense of trust and respect among individuals. Trust is essential for building and maintaining relationships, as it allows individuals to feel confident and secure in their interactions with others. When individuals trust and respect one another, they are more likely to feel supported and valued, which can strengthen their connections and lead to greater feelings of happiness and fulfillment. It is important for individuals to demonstrate trustworthiness and respect towards others, by honoring commitments, being reliable and consistent, and treating others with kindness and consideration.

In order to create a loving and nurturing environment, it is also important for individuals to practice self-care and self-compassion. Self-care involves taking care of one's physical, emotional, and mental well-being, by engaging in activities that promote health and happiness, such as exercise, meditation, hobbies, and socializing. Self-compassion involves treating oneself with kindness and understanding, and being forgiving and accepting of one's mistakes and shortcomings. When individuals practice self-care and self-compassion, they are better able to nurture themselves, and to offer love and care to others in a genuine and sustainable way. By fostering a sense of support, understanding, and acceptance, individuals can thrive and grow in a safe and nurturing environment, leading to greater happiness and fulfillment in their lives. It is important for individuals to prioritize creating and maintaining loving and nurturing environments in all aspects of their lives, in order to cultivate strong and healthy relationships, and to foster their own well-being and growth.

- Communicating effectively with your child

Communicating effectively with your child is an essential skill that all parents should strive to develop. Effective communication lays the foundation for a strong and healthy parent-child relationship, as well as promoting your child's emotional well-being and overall development. In this essay, we will explore the importance of effective communication with your child, discuss strategies for enhancing communication, and highlight the benefits of open and honest dialogue in the parent-child dynamic.

Effective communication with your child begins with active listening. Listening to your child without judgment or interruption shows them that their thoughts and feelings are valued and respected. By truly listening to your child, you can gain valuable insights into their emotions, experiences, and perspectives, which can help you better understand their needs and concerns. Active listening involves giving your full attention to your child, maintaining eye contact, and providing verbal and nonverbal cues to show that you are engaged in the conversation.

In addition to active listening, it is important to create a safe and supportive environment for your child to express themselves. Children are often hesitant to share their thoughts and feelings if they fear criticism, judgment, or punishment. By creating an open and non-judgmental space for communication, you encourage your child to be honest and forthcoming with their thoughts and emotions. This safe environment allows your child to feel comfortable sharing even their most challenging experiences and concerns, fostering a deeper bond and trust between you.

Another key aspect of effective communication with your child is using age-appropriate language and concepts. Tailoring your language and communication style to your child's developmental stage ensures that they can understand and engage with the conversation. For younger children, using simple and concrete language can help them grasp complex ideas and emotions. As your child grows, you can gradually introduce more abstract concepts and nuanced discussions to expand their communication skills and emotional intelligence.

Furthermore, it is important to be mindful of your nonverbal communication when interacting with your child. Nonverbal cues such as facial expressions, tone of voice, and body language can convey powerful messages that may contradict or enhance your verbal communication. By being aware of your nonverbal signals and ensuring they align with your verbal messages, you can enhance the clarity and effectiveness of your communication with your child.

In addition to actively listening and creating a supportive environment, affirming and validating your child's feelings and experiences can go a long way in strengthening your relationship. Acknowledging your child's emotions, even if you do not agree with them, shows that you respect their perspective and care about their well-being. Validating their feelings can help your child feel understood and accepted, fostering greater trust and openness in your communication.

Lastly, it is important to practice empathy and patience when communicating with your child. Empathy involves putting yourself in your child's shoes and understanding their emotions and experiences from their perspective. By empathizing with your child, you can better connect with them and respond to their needs in a caring and compassionate manner. Patience is also crucial when communicating with children, as they may take longer to express themselves or process information. By remaining patient and allowing your child the time and space to communicate at their own pace, you demonstrate your respect and support for their communication process. By practicing active listening, creating a safe and supportive environment, using age-appropriate language, being mindful of nonverbal cues, affirming and validating your child's feelings, and practicing empathy and patience, you can foster open and honest communication with your child. By prioritizing communication in your parent-child dynamic, you can strengthen your bond, build trust and understanding, and empower your child to express themselves authentically and confidently.

Chapter 3: Setting Boundaries and Discipline

- Establishing clear rules and consequences

Establishing clear rules and consequences is an essential aspect of maintaining order and discipline in any setting, whether it be a classroom, workplace, or community. By clearly outlining what is expected of individuals and the repercussions for failing to meet those expectations, organizations can create a structured environment that promotes accountability and responsibility.

One of the key benefits of establishing clear rules and consequences is that it provides a framework for behavior and decision-making. When individuals understand the boundaries and expectations that have been set, they are better equipped to make informed choices and act in a way that is consistent with the values and objectives of the organization. This can help to reduce confusion and ambiguity, ensuring that everyone is on the same page and working towards a common goal.

In addition to providing guidance for individuals, clear rules and consequences also serve as a form of protection for the organization. By clearly outlining what is considered acceptable behavior and the consequences for unacceptable actions, organizations can protect themselves from potential legal liabilities and disputes. This can help to minimize conflicts and ensure that everyone is treated fairly and consistently.

Furthermore, establishing clear rules and consequences can help to foster a sense of trust and respect within the organization. When individuals know that everyone is held accountable for their actions and that there are consequences for breaking the rules, it can create a culture of integrity and fairness. This can help to build relationships and promote a sense of community, as individuals come to trust that everyone is playing by the same set of rules.

When it comes to implementing clear rules and consequences, it is important to ensure that they are communicated effectively and consistently. This means that rules should be clearly written and easily accessible to all individuals within the organization. It is also important to ensure that consequences are fair and proportionate to the behavior in question, in order to maintain trust and credibility.

Additionally, it is important to ensure that rules are enforced consistently and fairly, in order to prevent any perception of favoritism or bias. This means that consequences should be applied consistently to all individuals, regardless of their position or relationship within the organization. By being transparent and consistent in the application of rules and consequences, organizations can create a culture of accountability and fairness that promotes trust and respect. By providing a framework for behavior and decision-making, organizations can create a structured environment that promotes accountability and responsibility. By communicating rules effectively, enforcing them consistently, and applying consequences fairly, organizations can build a culture of integrity and trust that fosters a sense of community and respect.

- Positive discipline techniques for behavior management

Positive discipline techniques are essential tools for educators and parents alike to effectively manage behavior in children. By using positive discipline strategies, adults can guide children in developing self-discipline, self-control, and problem-solving skills. This approach focuses on teaching children appropriate behaviors rather than punishing them for their mistakes. Positive discipline techniques encourage open communication, mutual respect, and cooperation between adults and children. By fostering a positive and supportive environment, adults can help children learn to make responsible choices and develop a strong sense of autonomy and self-esteem.

One of the key principles of positive discipline is setting clear and consistent boundaries. Children thrive on structure and routine, and setting clear expectations helps them understand what is expected of them. By establishing rules and consequences in advance, children know what behavior is acceptable and what is not. Consistency is crucial in enforcing these boundaries, as children need to know that rules will be consistently applied. This helps children feel secure and understand the consequences of their actions. Positive discipline techniques involve calmly and firmly enforcing rules without resorting to yelling, shaming, or physical punishment.

Another important aspect of positive discipline is building strong relationships with children based on trust and respect. When adults treat children with respect and empathy, children are more likely to listen and cooperate. Positive discipline techniques involve active listening, empathy, and understanding children's perspectives. By taking the time to validate children's feelings and emotions, adults can build trust and create a safe and supportive environment for children to express themselves. When children feel listened to and understood, they are more likely to cooperate and follow rules.

Positive discipline techniques also emphasize positive reinforcement and encouragement. Rather than focusing on negative behaviors, adults should praise and reward positive behaviors. By acknowledging and reinforcing good behavior, adults can motivate children to continue making positive choices. Positive reinforcement can take the form of verbal praise, rewards, or privileges. By focusing on the positive aspects of a child's behavior, adults can build children's confidence and self-esteem. This positive approach also helps children develop a growth mindset, where they see challenges as opportunities for learning and growth.

When children make mistakes or misbehave, adults should use positive discipline strategies to teach them appropriate behavior. Instead of punishment, adults can use natural consequences or logical consequences to help children understand the impact of their actions. Natural consequences are the natural result of a child's behavior, such as not wearing a jacket and getting cold. Logical consequences are imposed by adults to teach a lesson, such as cleaning up a mess that was made. By allowing children to experience the consequences of their actions, adults help them learn responsibility and accountability. It is important for adults to remain calm and patient during these teachable moments and provide guidance and support to help children learn from their mistakes. By using positive discipline strategies, adults can create a supportive and nurturing environment that promotes children's social, emotional, and cognitive development. Positive discipline helps children develop self-discipline, self-control, and problem-solving skills while building strong relationships based on trust and respect. By implementing positive discipline techniques consistently and compassionately, adults can help children grow into responsible, confident, and resilient individuals.

Chapter 4: Promoting Healthy Habits

- Encouraging good nutrition and physical activity

Encouraging good nutrition and physical activity is essential for promoting overall health and well-being. The benefits of healthy eating and regular exercise are numerous, including reduced risk of chronic diseases such as heart disease, diabetes, and certain types of cancer. In addition, proper nutrition and physical activity can help to maintain a healthy weight, improve mental health, and boost energy levels.

One of the key ways to encourage good nutrition is by promoting a balanced diet that includes a variety of foods from all the food groups. This means consuming plenty of fruits, vegetables, whole grains, lean proteins, and healthy fats. It is also important to limit foods that are high in added sugars, salt, and unhealthy fats. Educating individuals about the importance of nutrient-dense foods and providing them with resources, such as meal planning guides and recipes, can help them make healthier choices.

Physical activity is equally important for overall health and well-being. Regular exercise can help to strengthen muscles, improve cardiovascular health, and boost metabolism. It can also enhance mood, reduce stress, and improve sleep quality. Encouraging individuals to engage in a variety of physical activities, such as walking, jogging, swimming, and strength training, can help them find activities that they enjoy and are more likely to stick with long-term.

When it comes to promoting good nutrition and physical activity, it is important to take a holistic approach. This means addressing not only individual behaviors, but also the environmental and societal factors that can influence health. For example, access to healthy foods and safe spaces for physical activity can play a significant role in shaping individuals' choices and behaviors. By working to improve community resources, such as farmers' markets, community gardens, and recreational facilities, we can create environments that support healthy living for all.

In addition to providing education and resources, it is important to create a supportive and inclusive environment that encourages individuals to make positive changes to their diet and exercise habits. This may involve setting realistic goals, offering support and encouragement, and celebrating successes along the way. Group fitness classes, cooking demonstrations, and wellness challenges can also help to foster a sense of community and accountability among participants.

Ultimately, promoting good nutrition and physical activity is about empowering individuals to take control of their own health and well-being. By providing the necessary tools, resources, and support, we can help individuals make sustainable lifestyle changes that will benefit them in the long term. Encouraging a balanced approach to nutrition and physical activity can improve overall health, prevent chronic diseases, and enhance quality of life for individuals of all ages.

- Teaching hygiene and self-care skills

Teaching hygiene and self-care skills is an essential aspect of education that can have a profound impact on individuals' overall well-being and quality of life. Hygiene refers to practices that help maintain health and prevent the spread of illnesses, while self-care involves activities that individuals can do to take care of themselves both physically and mentally. By educating individuals on the importance of these skills and providing them with practical strategies for implementing them in their daily lives, educators can empower students to lead healthier and more fulfilling lives.

One of the key benefits of teaching hygiene and self-care skills is that it can help individuals develop a sense of personal responsibility for their own health and well-being. By instilling good hygiene habits early on, such as regularly washing hands, brushing teeth, and showering, individuals can reduce their risk of contracting illnesses and improve their overall health. Similarly, self-care activities like exercising, eating nutritious foods, and getting enough sleep can help individuals maintain a healthy lifestyle and manage stress more effectively.

By teaching these skills, educators can empower individuals to take control of their own health and make informed decisions about their well-being.

Furthermore, teaching hygiene and self-care skills can help individuals improve their self-esteem and confidence. When individuals take care of themselves and prioritize their health and well-being, they are more likely to feel good about themselves and have a positive self-image. By teaching individuals how to practice good hygiene and self-care, educators can help them develop a sense of self-worth and self-respect. This can have a ripple effect on other areas of their lives, as individuals who feel good about themselves are more likely to engage in positive social interactions, set and achieve goals, and cope with stress in a healthy way.

In addition to the physical and mental health benefits, teaching hygiene and self-care skills can also have a positive impact on individuals' social and emotional well-being. Good hygiene practices, such as showering regularly and wearing clean clothes, can help individuals feel more confident in social situations and improve their relationships with others. Similarly, self-care activities like mindfulness meditation and journaling can help individuals manage stress, improve their emotional regulation, and enhance their overall well-being. By teaching these skills, educators can help individuals develop the emotional intelligence and resilience they need to navigate life's challenges and build strong, supportive relationships with others.

Moreover, teaching hygiene and self-care skills can help individuals develop important life skills that are essential for success in school, work, and other areas of life. By teaching individuals how to maintain good hygiene and take care of themselves, educators can help them cultivate habits of discipline, organization, and self-control. These skills are not only important for maintaining good health, but also for achieving academic success, pursuing career goals, and building successful relationships. By teaching hygiene and self-care skills, educators can help individuals develop the foundational skills they need to thrive in all aspects of their lives. By educating individuals on the importance of these skills and providing them with practical strategies for implementing them in their daily lives, educators can empower students to lead healthier and more fulfilling lives. From improving physical and mental health to boosting self-esteem and developing important life skills, the benefits of teaching hygiene and self-care skills are vast and far-reaching. By prioritizing the teaching of these essential skills, educators can help individuals take control of their own health and well-being, build strong relationships with others, and achieve success in all areas of their lives.

Chapter 5: Fostering Emotional Intelligence

- Helping your child understand and manage their feelings

Helping children understand and manage their feelings is a crucial aspect of their emotional development. As children grow and navigate through the challenges of life, they will inevitably encounter a wide range of emotions, from happiness and excitement to anger and sadness. It is important for parents and caregivers to support children in understanding these feelings and learning how to effectively manage them. By doing so, children can develop emotional intelligence, resilience, and coping skills that will benefit them throughout their lives.

One of the first steps in helping children understand and manage their feelings is to create a safe and supportive environment where they feel comfortable expressing themselves. Children need to feel that their emotions are valid and that they will be listened to without judgment or criticism. This can be achieved by actively listening to children when they are expressing their feelings, acknowledging their emotions, and validating their experiences. By creating an open and accepting atmosphere, children will be more likely to communicate their feelings and seek guidance when needed.

It is also important to teach children about different emotions and help them recognize and label their feelings. This can be done through discussions about emotions, storytelling, and role-playing activities. By giving children the vocabulary to identify and express their emotions, they will be better equipped to understand and communicate their feelings in a healthy way. Additionally, parents and caregivers can model emotional intelligence by expressing their own feelings in a healthy and constructive manner, providing children with positive examples to follow.

Once children are able to recognize and label their emotions, the next step is to help them learn how to manage and regulate their feelings. This can be achieved through various strategies, such as deep breathing exercises, mindfulness techniques, and positive self-talk. Teaching children to take deep breaths when they are feeling overwhelmed or upset can help them calm down and regain control of their emotions. Similarly, practicing mindfulness can help children become more aware of their feelings and learn to respond to them in a more thoughtful and deliberate manner. Encouraging children to use positive self-talk, such as affirmations or encouraging statements, can also help them develop a more positive outlook and build resilience in the face of challenges.

In addition to teaching children coping strategies, it is important to help them develop healthy ways to express their feelings. Children may express their emotions through various means, such as through art, music, writing, or physical activity. Encouraging children to express themselves creatively can provide them with an outlet for their emotions and help them process their feelings in a constructive way. Parents and caregivers can also help children understand that it is okay to feel a range of emotions and that it is important to express them in a healthy and respectful manner.

Another important aspect of helping children understand and manage their feelings is teaching them problem-solving skills. Children will inevitably face challenges and obstacles that may trigger strong emotions, such as frustration, disappointment, or anger. By teaching children how to identify the underlying causes of their emotions and brainstorming solutions to address them, parents and caregivers can help children develop effective problem-solving skills. Encouraging children to think critically and consider different perspectives can help them develop resilience and adaptability in the face of adversity.

It is also important for parents and caregivers to provide consistent and nurturing support to children as they navigate their emotions. Children may experience a wide range of feelings throughout the day, and it is important for them to know that they can turn to their parents or caregivers for guidance and reassurance. By offering love, understanding, and empathy, parents and caregivers can help children feel secure and supported as they work through their emotions. Additionally, setting clear and consistent boundaries can help children feel safe and secure, providing them with a sense of stability and predictability in their lives. By creating a safe and supportive environment, teaching children about emotions, and providing them with coping strategies, parents and caregivers can help children build emotional intelligence, resilience, and coping skills that will benefit them throughout their lives. By fostering open communication, teaching problem-solving skills, and offering consistent support, parents and caregivers can help children navigate their emotions in a healthy and constructive manner. Ultimately, by empowering children to understand and manage their feelings, parents and caregivers can help them develop the emotional skills they need to thrive in today's complex and ever-changing world.

- Building resilience and coping skills

Resilience and coping skills are essential components of mental and emotional well-being. In today's fast-paced and often unpredictable world, the ability to bounce back from setbacks and adapt to challenging circumstances is more important than ever. Building resilience and coping skills can help individuals navigate life's ups and downs with grace and confidence, ultimately leading to a greater sense of overall happiness and fulfillment.

Resilience is the ability to withstand and recover from adversity, trauma, or stress. It involves a combination of mental, emotional, and social strength that allows individuals to maintain their well-being in the face of difficult circumstances. Coping skills, on the other hand, are specific strategies and techniques that individuals can use to manage stress, regulate emotions, and overcome obstacles. Together, resilience and coping skills form a powerful toolkit for navigating life's challenges and thriving in the face of adversity.

There are many factors that contribute to resilience and coping skills, including genetics, environment, and personal experiences. Some individuals may have a natural predisposition towards resilience, while others may need to work harder to develop these traits. Regardless of where one falls on the resilience spectrum, everyone has the capacity to strengthen their resilience and enhance their coping skills through intentional practice and self-awareness.

One of the key components of building resilience is developing a strong support network. Having friends, family, or other trusted individuals to turn to in times of need can provide a sense of security and comfort that enhances resilience.

Additionally, seeking out professional support through therapy or counseling can be beneficial for developing coping skills and building resilience. Therapists can provide guidance on effective coping strategies and help individuals process and heal from past traumas or stressors.

Another important aspect of building resilience is maintaining a positive mindset. Optimism, self-confidence, and a sense of purpose can all contribute to a resilient attitude that helps individuals overcome adversity. Engaging in activities that bring joy and fulfillment, such as hobbies, exercise, or creative pursuits, can also boost resilience and provide a healthy outlet for stress. Cultivating a sense of gratitude and mindfulness can further enhance resilience by fostering a sense of perspective and appreciation for life's blessings.

In addition to social support and a positive mindset, there are specific coping skills that individuals can cultivate to enhance their resilience. These skills include problem-solving, emotion regulation, and stress management techniques. Problem-solving skills involve breaking down complex problems into manageable steps and developing practical solutions. Emotion regulation skills help individuals identify and express their feelings in a healthy way, rather than bottling them up or lashing out inappropriately. Stress management techniques, such as deep breathing, meditation, or physical exercise, can help individuals relax and recharge in the face of overwhelming stressors.

It is important to remember that building resilience and coping skills is a lifelong process that requires dedication, effort, and self-reflection. It is normal to experience setbacks and challenges along the way, but these obstacles can provide valuable opportunities for growth and self-discovery. By actively working to enhance resilience and develop coping skills, individuals can cultivate a greater sense of inner strength, confidence, and well-being that will serve them well throughout their lives. By developing a strong support network, maintaining a positive mindset, and cultivating specific coping skills, individuals can enhance their ability to navigate life's challenges and thrive in the face of adversity. Through intentional practice and self-awareness, anyone can strengthen their resilience and build the resilience and coping skills necessary to flourish in even the most challenging circumstances.

Chapter 6: Supporting Academic Success

- Creating a positive learning environment at home

Creating a positive learning environment at home is essential for the academic and personal development of children. The home is where children spend a significant amount of time outside of school, and it plays a crucial role in shaping their attitudes towards learning and their overall academic success. A positive learning environment at home promotes a love for learning, encourages curiosity and creativity, and fosters a sense of independence and responsibility in children.

One of the first steps in creating a positive learning environment at home is establishing a routine and setting aside dedicated time for learning activities. Consistency is key in helping children feel safe, secure, and focused on their studies. Designating a specific study area in the home where children can work without distractions is also important. This area should be well-lit, comfortable, and stocked with all the necessary supplies such as pens, paper, textbooks, and reference materials. By creating a designated study space, children can associate this area with learning and focus, making it easier for them to concentrate and be productive.

In addition to having a dedicated study space, it is important for parents to be actively involved in their children's learning. This includes setting clear expectations and goals for academic achievement, providing encouragement and support, and offering assistance when needed. Parents can help their children with homework, engage in discussions about what they are learning in school, and provide opportunities for further exploration and enrichment. By showing an interest in their children's education and being actively involved in their learning, parents can create a positive and supportive learning environment at home.

Another key aspect of creating a positive learning environment at home is promoting a growth mindset in children. A growth mindset is the belief that intelligence and abilities can be developed through effort, perseverance, and feedback. By encouraging children to embrace challenges, learn from their mistakes, and see failure as an opportunity for growth, parents can help them develop resilience, motivation, and a love for learning. Parents can praise their children for their efforts and progress rather than just their achievements, and help them set realistic and achievable goals to work towards.

In addition to promoting a growth mindset, parents can also cultivate a love for learning by making it fun and engaging. This can be done through hands-on activities, educational games, puzzles, and experiments that spark curiosity and creativity. Parents can also incorporate real-world experiences and practical applications of what children are learning in school to make it more relevant and meaningful. By providing a variety of learning opportunities and making learning enjoyable, parents can help children develop a lifelong love for learning and a sense of curiosity and wonder about the world around them.

Creating a positive learning environment at home also involves fostering a sense of independence and responsibility in children. Parents can empower their children to take ownership of their education by encouraging them to set their own goals, manage their time effectively, and take initiative in their learning. This can be done by teaching children study skills, organization, and time management techniques, and by helping them develop a sense of accountability for their own learning. By giving children the tools and resources they need to succeed and by trusting them to make decisions and take control of their own learning, parents can help them develop the skills and habits they need to be successful in school and in life. By establishing a routine, setting aside dedicated time for learning, and creating a designated study space, parents can help children feel safe, secure, and focused on their studies. By being actively involved in their children's learning, promoting a growth mindset, making learning fun and engaging, and fostering independence and responsibility, parents can create a supportive and nurturing environment that encourages children to excel academically and develop a lifelong love for learning. With the right guidance and support from parents, children can thrive academically, emotionally, and socially, and reach their full potential.

- Tips for helping your child excel in school

As a parent, you play a crucial role in your child's education and overall success in school. By taking an active interest in your child's academic performance and providing them with the necessary support and guidance, you can help them excel in school and achieve their full potential. In this article, we will discuss a few tips and strategies that you can implement to support your child's academic development and foster a love for learning.

One of the most important ways you can help your child excel in school is by creating a positive and supportive learning environment at home. This means setting aside a dedicated study space for your child where they can focus and concentrate on their schoolwork. Make sure this space is free from distractions, such as television or loud noises, and is equipped with all the necessary supplies, such as paper, pencils, and books. By creating a designated study area, you can help your child develop good study habits and improve their concentration and focus.

Another important factor in helping your child excel in school is establishing a consistent routine and schedule. Help your child set aside specific times each day for studying, homework, and other school-related activities. By establishing a routine, you can help your child develop good time management skills and create a sense of structure and stability in their daily lives. Encourage your child to stick to this schedule as much as possible, but also be flexible and allow for breaks and downtime as needed. Consistency is key in helping your child stay on track and succeed academically.

In addition to establishing a positive learning environment and consistent routine, it is also important to communicate regularly with your child's teachers and stay informed about their progress in school. Attend parent-teacher conferences and other school events to stay up-to-date on your child's academic performance, behavior, and any areas that may need improvement. By building a strong relationship with your child's teachers, you can gain valuable insights into your child's strengths and weaknesses and work together to create a plan for academic success.

Furthermore, it is crucial to encourage your child to take an active role in their own learning and to develop a sense of ownership and responsibility for their academic success. Help your child set specific goals and objectives for each school year, semester, or quarter, and work with them to create a plan to achieve these goals. Encourage your child to track their progress and celebrate their accomplishments along the way. By empowering your child to take control of their own education, you can help them develop important skills, such as self-motivation, perseverance, and resilience, that will serve them well throughout their academic career.

Additionally, it is important to provide your child with the necessary support and resources to help them succeed in school. This may include hiring a tutor or enrolling your child in extracurricular activities or enrichment programs that can help them develop their skills and talents. Consider investing in educational materials, such as books, educational games, or online resources, that can help your child reinforce what they are learning in school and explore new subjects and interests. By providing your child with the tools they need to succeed, you can help them reach their full academic potential and excel in school. By creating a positive and supportive learning environment, establishing a consistent routine, communicating with your child's teachers, encouraging your child to take ownership of their education, and providing them with the necessary support and resources, you can help your child develop the skills and knowledge they need to succeed academically. Remember that every child is unique, and it may take some trial and error to find the strategies that work best for your child. Stay patient, persistent, and positive, and continue to support and encourage your child in their academic journey. With your help and guidance, your child can thrive in school and beyond.

Chapter 7: Encouraging Independence

- Teaching age-appropriate responsibilities

Teaching age-appropriate responsibilities to children is a crucial aspect of their development and growth. By instilling a sense of accountability and independence from a young age, children can learn valuable life skills that will serve them well in the future. It is important for parents and educators to understand the significance of assigning age-appropriate responsibilities, as well as how to do so effectively.

One of the key benefits of teaching age-appropriate responsibilities is that it helps children develop a sense of independence and autonomy. When children are given tasks and responsibilities that are suitable for their age and abilities, they learn to take ownership of their actions and make decisions on their own. This can help boost their self-esteem and confidence, as they see themselves as capable and competent individuals who are able to contribute to their families and communities.

Furthermore, teaching age-appropriate responsibilities helps children learn important life skills that will serve them well in adulthood. By assigning tasks such as cleaning their room, setting the table, or feeding pets, children learn the value of hard work, organization, and responsibility. These skills are essential for success in school, work, and relationships, and by learning them at a young age, children can develop good habits that will benefit them throughout their lives.

In addition, teaching age-appropriate responsibilities can help children cultivate a sense of empathy and compassion towards others. When children are responsible for tasks that benefit their family or community, such as helping with household chores or volunteering in their neighborhood, they learn to think beyond themselves and consider the needs of others. This can help instill values of kindness, generosity, and cooperation, and encourage children to become active and engaged members of their communities.

When assigning age-appropriate responsibilities to children, it is important for parents and educators to consider the child's age, abilities, and interests. Younger children may be given simple tasks such as putting away toys or helping with basic chores, while older children may be assigned more complex responsibilities such as cooking meals or caring for younger siblings. It is essential to provide clear instructions and guidance, as well as offer praise and encouragement for a job well done.

It is also important to involve children in the decision-making process when assigning responsibilities, as this can help them feel a sense of ownership and agency over their tasks. By discussing and negotiating responsibilities with children, parents and educators can help them understand the significance of their contributions and feel motivated to complete their tasks to the best of their abilities. Additionally, it is important to provide support and guidance as children learn new tasks, and to offer gentle reminders and assistance when needed. By instilling a sense of independence, responsibility, and empathy from a young age, children can learn valuable life skills that will benefit them throughout their lives. Parents and educators play a crucial role in guiding children towards age-appropriate responsibilities, and by providing clear instructions, support, and encouragement, they can help children develop the confidence and competence they need to succeed in the world.

- Allowing your child to make choices and learn from mistakes

Allowing your child to make choices and learn from mistakes is an essential aspect of their growth and development. As a parent, it is natural to want to protect your child from the hardships and difficulties of life. However, shielding them from making choices and learning from mistakes can hinder their ability to become independent, self-reliant individuals. By allowing your child to make choices, whether big or small, you are giving them the opportunity to develop critical thinking skills, problem-solving abilities, and decision-making capabilities. These skills are crucial for success in both academics and personal relationships.

When children are given the freedom to make their own choices, they are able to learn from their mistakes and failures. This process of trial and error is essential for growth and development. By allowing your child to experience the consequences of their decisions, they are able to gain a deeper understanding of cause and effect. This can help them develop a sense of accountability and responsibility for their actions. When children are shielded from making choices and mistakes, they may struggle to take responsibility for their own behavior and actions in the future.

It is important for parents to create a safe and supportive environment for their children to make choices and learn from their mistakes. This means providing guidance and support when needed, but also allowing your child the freedom to make their own decisions. It can be helpful to have conversations with your child about the choices they are making and the potential consequences of those choices. By fostering open communication and mutual respect, you can help your child develop the confidence and self-assurance needed to navigate life's challenges.

It is also important for parents to model positive behavior and decision-making skills for their children. Children learn by example, so it is crucial for parents to demonstrate the importance of making thoughtful and responsible choices. By showing your child how to approach decision-making with a clear and rational mindset, you are helping them develop the skills they need to make informed choices in the future. This can also help your child develop a sense of self-confidence and self-reliance, as they learn to trust their own judgment and intuition. By giving your child the freedom to make decisions, you are helping them develop critical thinking skills, problem-solving abilities, and decision-making capabilities. It is important for parents to create a safe and supportive environment for their children to learn from their mistakes and failures. By fostering open communication, mutual respect, and positive role modeling, parents can help their children develop the confidence and self-assurance needed to navigate life's challenges. Ultimately, the ability to make choices and learn from mistakes is an essential skill that will benefit your child throughout their lives.

Chapter 8: Strengthening Family Relationships

- Building strong bonds with siblings and extended family

Building strong bonds with siblings and extended family members is a crucial aspect of maintaining harmonious relationships within the family unit. Siblings play a unique role in our lives, as they are often our first friends and confidants. Extended family members, such as aunts, uncles, cousins, and grandparents, also contribute to the richness of our family experiences. It is important to cultivate these relationships, as they provide support, love, and a sense of belonging that can last a lifetime.

One of the key elements in building strong bonds with siblings and extended family members is communication. Communication is the cornerstone of any healthy relationship, and it is vital to express your thoughts, feelings, and needs openly and honestly. By communicating effectively with your siblings and extended family members, you can build trust, understanding, and mutual respect. This can help to prevent misunderstandings and conflicts from arising, and ensure that your relationships remain strong and supportive.

Spending quality time together is another important factor in strengthening bonds with siblings and extended family members. Whether it is through shared activities, family gatherings, or regular phone calls and video chats, making an effort to connect with your loved ones on a regular basis can help to deepen your relationships. These shared experiences can create lasting memories and strengthen the bonds that you share with your siblings and extended family members.

It is also important to show appreciation and gratitude towards your siblings and extended family members. These individuals play a significant role in your life, and it is essential to acknowledge the love, support, and care that they provide. Expressing gratitude through kind words, gestures, or small acts of kindness can go a long way in showing your appreciation for the important role that your siblings and extended family members play in your life.

Building strong bonds with siblings and extended family members also involves resolving conflicts and disagreements in a healthy and constructive manner. Conflict is a natural part of any relationship, but it is important to address issues openly and respectfully. By listening to each other's perspectives, working towards finding a compromise, and seeking solutions together, you can strengthen your relationships and build a stronger, more resilient bond with your siblings and extended family members.

Additionally, it is important to respect the individual differences and boundaries of your siblings and extended family members. Each person is unique, with their own thoughts, feelings, and preferences. By respecting these differences and understanding each other's boundaries, you can foster a sense of acceptance, trust, and mutual understanding within your family relationships. This can help to create a supportive and loving environment where everyone feels valued and respected.

Lastly, it is important to be there for your siblings and extended family members during both good times and bad. Life is full of ups and downs, and it is important to be a source of support, comfort, and encouragement for your loved ones when they need it most. Whether it is celebrating their achievements, offering a listening ear during difficult times, or providing a helping hand when they are in need, being there for your siblings and extended family members can help to strengthen your relationships and create lasting bonds that will stand the test of time. By communicating effectively, spending quality time together, showing appreciation and gratitude, resolving conflicts in a healthy manner, respecting individual differences, and being there for each other during both good times and bad, you can foster meaningful and lasting relationships with your loved ones. These bonds can provide a sense of security, love, and belonging that can enrich your life and bring joy and fulfillment to your family relationships.

- Planning quality family time together

In today's fast-paced and technology-driven world, it can be easy for families to become disconnected and overwhelmed with their busy schedules. However, it is crucial for families to prioritize quality time together in order to build strong bonds and create lasting memories. Family time is not just about being physically present in the same space, but it is about engaging with one another, communicating effectively, and fostering a sense of closeness and connection.

One of the first steps in planning quality family time is to establish a routine or schedule that works for everyone in the family. This can involve setting aside designated times each week for family activities, meals, or outings. By creating a routine, families can ensure that they have dedicated time to spend together and can avoid conflicts or distractions that may arise from conflicting schedules. By making family time a priority and scheduling it into their routine, families can ensure that they are able to consistently connect and bond with one another.

Another important aspect of planning quality family time is to choose activities that are engaging and enjoyable for everyone involved. This can involve a variety of activities, such as playing games, cooking together, going for a walk or hike, or watching a movie. By choosing activities that everyone in the family enjoys, families can ensure that their time together is meaningful and rewarding. It is also important to consider the interests and preferences of each family member in order to create a balance of activities that appeal to everyone.

Communication is key when it comes to planning quality family time. Families should make an effort to communicate openly and honestly with one another, expressing their needs and desires for family time. By having open and honest communication, families can ensure that everyone's expectations are met and that conflicts or misunderstandings are avoided. It is important for families to prioritize clear and effective communication in order to make the most of their time together and to strengthen their relationships.

In addition to setting aside designated time for family activities and choosing engaging and enjoyable activities, families can also benefit from unplugging and taking a break from technology during their family time. In today's digital age, it can be easy for families to become consumed by screens and devices, which can detract from their ability to connect and engage with one another. By unplugging from technology and focusing on each other during family time, families can create a more meaningful and enriching experience that fosters deeper connections and strengthens their relationships.

Finding opportunities to create lasting memories is another important aspect of planning quality family time together. Whether it is taking a family vacation, celebrating special occasions, or participating in traditions and rituals, creating memories together can help to solidify bonds and create a sense of unity and belonging within the family. By making an effort to create lasting memories, families can look back on their time together with fondness and nostalgia, creating a sense of shared history and connection.

Ultimately, planning quality family time is essential for building strong relationships, fostering communication, and creating lasting memories. By setting aside dedicated time for family activities, choosing engaging and enjoyable activities, prioritizing open and honest communication, unplugging from technology, and creating lasting memories, families can ensure that their time together is meaningful, rewarding, and fulfilling. By making family time a priority and actively planning and engaging in quality activities together, families can strengthen their bonds and create a sense of unity and connectedness that will endure for years to come.

Chapter 9: Managing Screen Time and Technology

- Setting limits on electronic devices

Setting limits on electronic devices has become an increasingly important issue in today's society. With the rise of smartphones, tablets, and laptops, it has become all too easy for individuals to become engrossed in their devices, often to the detriment of their physical and mental well-being. Research has shown that excessive screen time can lead to a host of negative consequences, including poor sleep quality, decreased physical activity, and increased risk of mental health issues such as anxiety and depression.

In order to mitigate these risks, it is important for individuals to set limits on their electronic device usage. This can be challenging, especially in a world where technology is ubiquitous and constantly demanding our attention. However, by establishing clear boundaries and sticking to them, individuals can take steps to protect themselves from the harmful effects of excessive screen time.

One common approach to setting limits on electronic devices is to establish designated "tech-free" zones and times. For example, individuals may choose to ban electronic devices from the bedroom in order to promote better sleep hygiene. Similarly, setting aside specific times of day where devices are not allowed can help individuals to create a healthy balance between screen time and other activities.

Another effective strategy for setting limits on electronic devices is to utilize the built-in tools and features that many devices offer for managing screen time. For example, smartphones and tablets often have settings that allow users to set time limits for specific apps or to schedule "downtime" periods where certain apps are disabled. By taking advantage of these features, individuals can proactively manage their device usage and prevent themselves from falling into the trap of mindlessly scrolling or tapping away.

It is also important for individuals to be mindful of their own device usage habits and how they may be impacting their overall well-being. By being aware of how much time is spent on devices each day, individuals can make more informed decisions about when and where it is appropriate to set limits. Additionally, taking regular breaks from screens and engaging in other activities, such as exercise, reading, or spending time with loved ones, can help to counteract the negative effects of excessive screen time. By establishing clear boundaries, utilizing device management tools, and being mindful of device usage habits, individuals can protect themselves from the negative consequences of excessive screen time and promote their overall well-being. By taking proactive steps to manage device usage, individuals can enjoy the benefits of technology without falling prey to its potential pitfalls.

- Promoting balance and healthy use of technology

Technology has become an integral part of our daily lives, offering many benefits and conveniences. However, with the increasing reliance on technology, it is important to promote a balance and healthy use of technology in order to prevent negative consequences on physical, mental, and emotional well-being. In today's digital age, it is crucial for individuals to be mindful of their technology usage and make conscious efforts to create healthy habits when it comes to their digital devices.

One of the key ways to promote balance and healthy use of technology is by setting boundaries and limits on screen time. Excessive screen time has been linked to a variety of health issues, including eye strain, poor posture, and disrupted sleep patterns. By setting limits on the amount of time spent on devices, individuals can reduce the potential negative impacts of excessive screen time and create a healthier relationship with technology. This can be achieved by setting specific time limits for device usage, scheduling regular breaks from screens, and establishing tech-free zones in the home.

In addition to setting limits on screen time, it is also important to be mindful of the quality of technology use. Instead of mindlessly scrolling through social media or binge-watching videos, individuals should aim to engage with technology in a purposeful and intentional manner. This could involve using technology for educational purposes, such as learning a new skill or connecting with others through online communities.

Another important aspect of promoting balance and healthy use of technology is practicing digital detoxing. Just as our bodies need a break from certain foods or substances, our minds also benefit from periodic breaks from technology. A digital detox involves taking a temporary break from all digital devices, such as smartphones, computers, and tablets. This break allows individuals to recharge, reconnect with the physical world, and gain perspective on their relationship with technology. By incorporating regular digital detoxes into their routine, individuals can reduce feelings of overwhelm and burnout associated with constant connectivity.

Furthermore, fostering a healthy relationship with technology also involves practicing mindfulness and self-awareness. This means being aware of how technology is impacting one's thoughts, emotions, and behaviors, and making conscious choices to promote a healthy balance. Mindfulness techniques, such as meditation and deep breathing exercises, can help individuals become more attuned to their technology usage and make more intentional decisions about when and how to engage with digital devices. By practicing mindfulness, individuals can cultivate a greater sense of awareness and self-regulation when it comes to their technology use.

It is also important to seek support and guidance when navigating the complexities of technology use. This could involve reaching out to mental health professionals, technology addiction specialists, or support groups for assistance in managing technology usage. By seeking help from knowledgeable sources, individuals can gain valuable insights and strategies for promoting a healthy balance with technology. Additionally, discussing concerns and challenges related to technology use with friends, family members, or colleagues can provide a sense of validation and support in developing healthier technology habits. By taking proactive steps to prioritize well-being over constant connectivity, individuals can enjoy the benefits of technology while also maintaining a healthy balance in their lives.

Chapter 10: Handling Challenging Behaviors

- Strategies for dealing with defiance and tantrums

Defiance and tantrums are common behaviors exhibited by young children as they navigate through the developmental stages of growing up. It is important for parents and caregivers to understand that these behaviors are a natural part of a child's development and should be approached with patience and understanding. In this article, we will explore strategies for dealing with defiance and tantrums in a positive and constructive manner.

One of the key strategies for dealing with defiance and tantrums is to set clear and consistent boundaries for your child. Children thrive in an environment that provides structure and routine, so it is important to establish rules and expectations for behavior early on. By clearly outlining what is acceptable and unacceptable behavior, you are setting the stage for your child to understand the consequences of their actions.

It is also important to remain calm and composed when faced with defiance and tantrums. Children look to their parents and caregivers for guidance and reassurance, so it is important to model positive behavior in times of stress. Taking deep breaths and counting to ten can help you stay calm and respond to your child in a measured and controlled manner.

Another effective strategy for dealing with defiance and tantrums is to validate your child's feelings. It is important to acknowledge and validate your child's emotions, even if you do not agree with their behavior. By acknowledging their feelings, you are showing your child that you understand and empathize with them, which can help defuse the situation and prevent escalation.

It is also important to use positive reinforcement when dealing with defiance and tantrums. Praising your child for good behavior and offering rewards for following rules can help encourage them to exhibit positive behaviors in the future. Positive reinforcement is a powerful tool for shaping behavior and can help your child learn to make better choices.

In addition to positive reinforcement, it is important to use effective communication techniques when dealing with defiance and tantrums. It is important to communicate clearly and calmly with your child, explaining why their behavior is unacceptable and what the consequences will be if they continue to act out. Using age-appropriate language and speaking in a calm and respectful tone can help your child understand the impact of their actions.

It is also important to be consistent in your approach to dealing with defiance and tantrums. Children thrive on routine and predictability, so it is important to set clear boundaries and consistently enforce them. By being consistent, you are sending a clear message to your child about what is expected of them, which can help prevent future outbursts.

In a nutshell, it is important to seek support and guidance when dealing with defiance and tantrums. Parenting can be challenging, and it is important to reach out to friends, family, or a professional for advice and support. Seeking help can help you navigate through the ups and downs of parenting and learn new strategies for dealing with defiance and tantrums. By setting clear boundaries, remaining calm and composed, validating your child's feelings, using positive reinforcement, effective communication techniques, being consistent, and seeking support, you can effectively deal with defiance and tantrums in a positive and constructive manner. Parenting is a journey filled with ups and downs, but by approaching challenging behaviors with patience and understanding, you can help your child navigate through the developmental stages of growing up with confidence and resilience.

- Seeking support for complex behavior issues

Behavior issues can be challenging to navigate, particularly when they are complex in nature. These issues can arise in various settings, such as in schools, at work, or at home, and can impact an individual's overall well-being and functioning. Seeking support for complex behavior issues is crucial in order to address the underlying causes and implement effective strategies for managing and improving behavior.

When it comes to seeking support for complex behavior issues, it is important to first understand the underlying factors that may be contributing to the behavior. This may involve conducting a thorough assessment to identify any potential triggers, patterns, or underlying mental health issues that may be influencing the behavior. By gaining a better understanding of the root causes of the behavior, it is possible to develop more targeted interventions that address these underlying issues.

One of the key aspects of seeking support for complex behavior issues is collaborating with a team of professionals who have expertise in behavior management and intervention. This may include psychologists, behavior analysts, social workers, teachers, or other professionals who can offer specialized knowledge and skills in addressing behavior issues. By working together as a team, it is possible to develop comprehensive and effective strategies for managing and improving behavior.

In addition to working with a team of professionals, it is also important to involve the individual affected by the behavior issues in the process of seeking support. This may involve engaging in open and honest discussions about the behavior, as well as exploring the individual's own perspectives and insights into their behavior. By involving the individual in the process, it is possible to develop interventions that are more tailored to their specific needs and preferences.

Another important aspect of seeking support for complex behavior issues is utilizing evidence-based practices and interventions. This involves relying on research-backed strategies and techniques that have been shown to be effective in managing behavior issues. By incorporating evidence-based practices into interventions, it is possible to increase the likelihood of success and improve outcomes for individuals struggling with complex behavior issues.

In addition to utilizing evidence-based practices, it is also important to regularly evaluate and monitor the effectiveness of interventions for complex behavior issues. This may involve tracking progress, gathering feedback from individuals and team members, and making adjustments as needed to ensure that interventions remain effective and relevant. By staying vigilant and proactive in monitoring interventions, it is possible to make continuous improvements and optimize outcomes for individuals seeking support for complex behavior issues.

Ultimately, seeking support for complex behavior issues is a collaborative and ongoing process that requires patience, creativity, and dedication. By working together as a team, involving the individual in the process, utilizing evidence-based practices, and monitoring interventions regularly, it is possible to develop effective strategies for managing and improving behavior. With the right guidance and support, individuals struggling with complex behavior issues can overcome challenges and achieve positive outcomes.

Chapter 11: Nurturing Creativity and Imagination

- Providing opportunities for artistic expression

Artistic expression is a fundamental component of human communication, allowing individuals to convey thoughts, emotions, and experiences through various mediums such as painting, music, dance, theater, and literature. Providing opportunities for artistic expression is essential for fostering creativity, self-expression, and personal growth. It allows individuals to explore their creativity, develop their talents, and express themselves in ways that words alone cannot capture.

Artistic expression can provide a powerful outlet for emotions, enabling individuals to process and communicate complex feelings that may be difficult to express verbally. Through art, individuals can explore their innermost thoughts and emotions, gaining insight into their own experiences and finding ways to cope with challenging emotions. For example, painting can be a cathartic way to release pent-up feelings, while music can provide comfort and solace during times of distress. By providing opportunities for artistic expression, we can empower individuals to navigate their emotions in a healthy and constructive manner.

Furthermore, artistic expression can be a valuable tool for building self-confidence and self-esteem. Engaging in artistic activities allows individuals to develop their skills, hone their talents, and showcase their unique abilities. By celebrating their creative achievements, individuals can gain a sense of accomplishment and pride in their work, boosting their self-confidence and self-worth. This can be particularly beneficial for individuals who may struggle with low self-esteem or insecurity, providing them with a platform to showcase their talents and receive positive feedback and validation.

In addition, providing opportunities for artistic expression can foster a sense of community and connection among individuals. Art has a universal language that transcends cultural and linguistic barriers, enabling people from diverse backgrounds to come together and connect through shared creative experiences. Collaborative art projects, such as group painting sessions or musical performances, can encourage teamwork, cooperation, and mutual respect among participants. By creating a sense of belonging and camaraderie, artistic expression can help individuals forge meaningful relationships and build strong social connections.

Moreover, artistic expression can be a powerful tool for promoting cultural diversity, understanding, and tolerance. Through art, individuals can explore different perspectives, traditions, and ways of life, gaining a deeper appreciation for the diversity of human experience. By encouraging individuals to engage with art from various cultures and backgrounds, we can promote empathy, understanding, and respect for others. This can help break down stereotypes and prejudices, fostering a more inclusive and tolerant society where individuals from all walks of life can come together and celebrate their shared humanity. By offering platforms and resources for individuals to engage in artistic activities, we can empower them to explore their creativity, express their emotions, build self-confidence, connect with others, and promote cultural understanding. Artistic expression has the power to transform lives, inspire change, and create a more vibrant and harmonious society. It is essential that we continue to support and celebrate the arts, recognizing the profound impact that artistic expression can have on individuals and communities alike.

- Encouraging imaginative play and exploration

Imaginative play and exploration are crucial aspects of childhood development, helping children to better understand the world around them, develop important social and cognitive skills, and foster creativity and problem-solving abilities. As educators, parents, and caregivers, it is essential that we encourage and support children in engaging in imaginative play and exploration in order to promote their overall growth and development. By creating environments that facilitate such activities and providing children with the time, resources, and encouragement they need, we can help them to thrive and reach their full potential.

One of the key benefits of imaginative play and exploration is the development of creativity. When children engage in imaginative play, they are able to explore different scenarios, roles, and perspectives, which can help to stimulate their creativity and imagination. Through pretending to be someone else or something else, children can expand their thinking, problem-solving skills, and ability to think outside the box. By encouraging children to use their imaginations and explore new ideas, we are helping them to develop the skills they need to be successful in an ever-changing and competitive world.

In addition to fostering creativity, imaginative play and exploration can also help children to develop important social skills. When children engage in pretend play with others, they are able to practice important social and emotional skills such as cooperation, communication, and empathy. By working together to create and act out different scenarios, children learn to take on different roles, share ideas, and collaborate with their peers. This type of play can help children to develop strong relationships with others, build their self-confidence, and learn how to navigate social situations in a positive and constructive manner.

Furthermore, imaginative play and exploration can also help children to develop important cognitive skills. By engaging in pretend play, children are able to exercise their critical thinking skills, problem-solving abilities, and decision-making processes. Through exploring new ideas, experimenting with different scenarios, and trying out various solutions, children can learn important cognitive skills that will help them to succeed in school and life. By providing children with opportunities to engage in imaginative play and exploration, we are helping them to develop the cognitive skills they need to think critically, solve problems, and make informed decisions.

It is important for educators, parents, and caregivers to create environments that support imaginative play and exploration. This can be done by providing children with access to a variety of materials, toys, and props that can be used in pretend play, such as dress-up clothes, blocks, art supplies, and pretend food. By offering children a diverse range of resources and opportunities for creative expression, we are helping to foster their imagination, curiosity, and sense of wonder. Additionally, it is important for adults to provide children with the time, space, and support they need to engage in imaginative play and exploration. By setting aside dedicated time for play, encouraging children to explore their interests, and participating in play alongside them, adults can help to nurture children's creativity and curiosity. By encouraging children to engage in pretend play, providing them with the resources they need, and creating supportive environments that facilitate such activities, we can help children to thrive and reach their full potential. As educators, parents, and caregivers, it is our responsibility to prioritize imaginative play and exploration in our interactions with children, as it is through these activities that children can learn, grow, and develop into well-rounded individuals. By valuing and promoting imaginative play and exploration, we are laying the foundation for children's future success and well-being.

Chapter 12: Dealing with Special Needs and Differences

- Advocating for your child's unique needs

Advocating for your child's unique needs is an important aspect of parenting that can have a significant impact on their overall well-being and success. As a parent, you are your child's greatest advocate and it is essential that you understand how to effectively navigate the complex systems and resources available to ensure that your child receives the support and accommodations they require. This process can be daunting and overwhelming, but with the right knowledge and tools, you can confidently advocate for your child and help them thrive.

The first step in advocating for your child's unique needs is to educate yourself about their specific challenges and strengths. This requires open communication with your child, their teachers, medical professionals, and any other relevant stakeholders. By gaining a thorough understanding of your child's needs, you can better tailor your advocacy efforts to address their unique circumstances. It is also important to stay informed about the laws and regulations that govern special education and disability services, as this knowledge will ensure that you are able to effectively advocate for your child within the legal framework.

One of the most important aspects of advocating for your child's unique needs is building a strong support network. This network can include family members, friends, teachers, therapists, and other professionals who can provide guidance, advice, and support as you navigate the advocacy process. By surrounding yourself with knowledgeable and empathetic individuals, you can gain valuable insights and perspectives that will help you advocate for your child more effectively.

Another crucial aspect of advocating for your child's unique needs is developing a clear and comprehensive plan of action. This plan should outline the specific goals and objectives you hope to achieve, as well as the strategies and resources you will use to accomplish them. By establishing a well-defined plan, you can keep track of your progress, stay organized, and ensure that you are making informed decisions that are in the best interest of your child.

In advocating for your child's unique needs, it is important to remember that you are not alone. There are a wealth of resources available to support parents in their advocacy efforts, including advocacy organizations, support groups, and online forums where you can connect with other parents facing similar challenges. By leveraging these resources, you can gain valuable support, advice, and guidance that will empower you to advocate for your child effectively and confidently.

It is also important to remember that advocating for your child's unique needs is a continuous process that requires ongoing dedication and commitment. As your child grows and their needs evolve, you may need to adjust your advocacy efforts to ensure that they continue to receive the support and accommodations they require. By staying informed, building a strong support network, developing a clear plan of action, and leveraging available resources, you can effectively advocate for your child and help them reach their full potential.

- Finding resources and support for children with disabilities

Children with disabilities often require additional resources and support to help them reach their full potential and thrive in various aspects of their lives. These resources can include educational support, therapeutic services, assistive technology, and community programs geared towards children with disabilities. Finding the right resources and support for a child with disabilities can be a daunting task for parents and caregivers, but it is crucial for the child's overall well-being and development.

One of the first steps in finding resources and support for children with disabilities is to learn about the specific needs of the child. Each child is unique, and their disabilities may require different types of support. It is important to work closely with healthcare professionals, therapists, and educators to assess the child's strengths and areas that need support. This information can help guide the search for resources and support that are tailored to the child's individual needs.

Another important aspect of finding resources and support for children with disabilities is to research and connect with organizations and agencies that specialize in providing services for children with disabilities. These organizations can offer a wealth of information, support, and resources that can help parents and caregivers navigate the complex system of support services available for children with disabilities. Some examples of such organizations include non-profit organizations, advocacy groups, and government agencies that focus on children with disabilities.

Educational support is often a critical component of a child's development and success. Children with disabilities may require specialized educational services, such as individualized education plans (IEPs) or accommodations in the classroom. Parents and caregivers can work with the child's school to develop an IEP that outlines the child's specific needs and goals, as well as the support services and accommodations that will help them succeed academically. It is important for parents to be informed about their child's rights under special education laws, such as the Individuals with Disabilities Education Act (IDEA), and to advocate for the services and supports that their child needs to thrive in school.

Therapeutic services are also essential for many children with disabilities to help them overcome challenges and reach their full potential. Therapies such as physical therapy, occupational therapy, speech therapy, and behavioral therapy can be instrumental in helping children with disabilities develop essential skills and abilities. It is important for parents and caregivers to find qualified and experienced therapists who specialize in working with children with disabilities and who can tailor their services to meet the child's specific needs.

Assistive technology is another valuable resource for children with disabilities. Assistive technology includes tools and devices that help children with disabilities communicate, learn, and perform everyday tasks more independently. Examples of assistive technology include communication devices, adaptive equipment, and software programs designed for children with disabilities.

Parents and caregivers can work with therapists, educators, and assistive technology specialists to identify the tools and devices that will best support the child's needs and enhance their quality of life.

In addition to professional services and resources, community programs can also play a vital role in supporting children with disabilities. Community programs such as support groups, recreational activities, and social skills groups can provide children with disabilities with opportunities to connect with peers, build social skills, and engage in meaningful activities. Parents and caregivers can research local community programs and organizations that offer services for children with disabilities and explore opportunities for their child to participate in activities that align with their interests and needs.

It is important for parents and caregivers to remember that they are not alone in their journey to find resources and support for children with disabilities. Building a strong support network of professionals, organizations, and other families with children with disabilities can provide valuable guidance, information, and emotional support. Parents can also reach out to their child's healthcare providers, therapists, and educators for recommendations and referrals to resources and support services. By actively seeking out and utilizing available resources and support, parents and caregivers can help their child with disabilities thrive and reach their full potential.

Chapter 13: Cultivating Gratitude and Positivity

- Practicing gratitude and mindfulness as a family

Gratitude and mindfulness are two powerful practices that can greatly enhance the well-being and happiness of individuals, couples, and families. When these practices are incorporated into daily life, they can have a profound impact on the overall quality of relationships and communication within the family unit. In this essay, we will explore the benefits of practicing gratitude and mindfulness as a family, as well as provide practical tips on how to incorporate these practices into your daily routine.

Gratitude is the practice of acknowledging and appreciating the positive aspects of life, no matter how big or small. When we express gratitude, we are cultivating a sense of abundance and positivity which can have a ripple effect on those around us. In a family setting, practicing gratitude can help to foster stronger bonds and create a more harmonious environment. By expressing gratitude towards one another, family members can feel valued and appreciated, which can lead to increased feelings of love and connection.

One way to incorporate gratitude into your family life is to start a gratitude journal. This can be a shared journal where each family member takes turns writing down things they are grateful for each day. This practice can help to shift the focus from what is lacking in life to what is abundant, fostering a sense of contentment and appreciation within the family unit. Another way to practice gratitude as a family is to engage in gratitude exercises, such as going around the dinner table and sharing one thing you are grateful for each day. This simple practice can help to create a positive and uplifting atmosphere within the family.

Mindfulness is the practice of being fully present in the moment, without judgment. When we practice mindfulness, we are able to fully experience and appreciate the present moment, rather than worrying about the future or ruminating on the past. In a family setting, practicing mindfulness can help to improve communication, reduce conflict, and foster a sense of connection and intimacy. By practicing mindfulness as a family, you can create a space where each family member feels seen, heard, and valued.

One way to incorporate mindfulness into your family life is to practice mindful eating together. This can involve taking the time to fully experience and savor each bite of food, paying attention to the taste, texture, and aroma of the meal. By practicing mindful eating as a family, you can create a sense of presence and connection around the dinner table. Another way to practice mindfulness as a family is to engage in mindful activities together, such as going for a walk in nature or practicing yoga. These activities can help to cultivate a sense of calm and connection within the family unit. By incorporating these practices into your daily routine, you can create a more harmonious and loving family environment, where each member feels valued and appreciated. So why not start incorporating gratitude and mindfulness into your family life today. Your family will thank you for it.

- Teaching your child the importance of a positive attitude

Teaching your child the importance of a positive attitude is essential for their overall well-being and success in life. A positive attitude can help children navigate challenges, overcome setbacks, and build resilience to face the ups and downs of life. It is a valuable skill that can have a profound impact on their mental health, relationships, and academic performance. As parents, it is our responsibility to instill this mindset in our children from a young age so that they can grow into confident, optimistic individuals.

One of the most effective ways to teach your child the importance of a positive attitude is by modeling it yourself. Children learn by observing and imitating their parents, so it is crucial to demonstrate positivity in your own words and actions. Show them how to tackle challenges with a can-do attitude, how to find the silver lining in difficult situations, and how to approach life with optimism and resilience. By being a positive role model, you can set a powerful example for your child to follow.

Another key aspect of teaching your child the importance of a positive attitude is to encourage them to practice gratitude and mindfulness. Help them develop a habit of expressing gratitude for the good things in their life, no matter how big or small. Encourage them to keep a gratitude journal or simply take a moment each day to reflect on the positive aspects of their day. By focusing on what they have rather than what they lack, children can cultivate a more positive outlook on life.

In addition, teaching your child the importance of a positive attitude involves helping them develop a growth mindset. A growth mindset is the belief that abilities and intelligence can be developed through effort and perseverance. By teaching your child to view challenges as opportunities for growth and learning, you can help them build resilience and cope with setbacks more effectively. Encourage them to embrace mistakes as learning opportunities, and praise their efforts and progress rather than just their achievements.

Furthermore, it is important to emphasize the power of positive thinking and self-talk in shaping a child's attitude. Teach your child to recognize negative thoughts and replace them with positive affirmations. Encourage them to visualize success, set goals, and believe in their ability to achieve them. By fostering a positive internal dialogue, you can empower your child to overcome self-doubt and develop a strong sense of self-esteem. By modeling positivity, practicing gratitude and mindfulness, promoting a growth mindset, and encouraging positive thinking and self-talk, you can help your child develop the skills and mindset they need to thrive in life. Remember that building a positive attitude is a lifelong journey, and it is never too early or too late to start instilling this mindset in your child. By taking the time to teach and nurture positivity in your child, you are setting them up for a brighter and more fulfilling future.

Chapter 14: Connecting with Other Parents

- Building a support network of fellow parents

Building a support network of fellow parents is essential for navigating the challenges and joys of raising children. Parenting can be an overwhelming experience, and having a group of individuals who can offer advice, understanding, and encouragement can make a significant difference in the journey. Connecting with other parents also provides an opportunity for sharing experiences, learning from each other, and forming meaningful relationships that can last a lifetime.

One of the first steps in building a support network of fellow parents is to seek out like-minded individuals who share similar values and parenting styles. This can be done through parent groups, online forums, parenting classes, or community events. By connecting with others who are facing similar challenges, parents can find comfort in knowing they are not alone and can benefit from the wisdom and perspective of others who have been in their shoes.

In addition to seeking out other parents, it is important to foster relationships with individuals who can offer different perspectives and experiences. Diversity within a support network can be incredibly valuable, as it can provide a range of opinions and ideas that can help parents see situations from different angles. By engaging with individuals who come from diverse backgrounds and have varying parenting styles, parents can expand their knowledge and understanding of different approaches to parenting.

Once a support network has been established, it is important to nurture and maintain these relationships. This can be done by regular communication, whether in person, through phone calls, or online. Setting up regular meetings or playdates can provide opportunities to connect and share experiences. Additionally, offering support to other parents in the network can strengthen bonds and create a sense of reciprocity within the group.

Building a support network of fellow parents can also provide a wealth of resources and information. Parents in a support network can share recommendations for childcare providers, schools, pediatricians, and other services that may be helpful in raising children. They can also offer practical advice on managing various parenting challenges, such as sleep training, discipline strategies, and managing sibling rivalry. By pooling their knowledge and resources, parents can create a supportive community that can help each other navigate the ups and downs of parenthood.

In addition to providing practical support, a network of fellow parents can also offer emotional support. Parenting can be a rollercoaster of emotions, from joy and pride to frustration and exhaustion. Having a group of individuals who can empathize with your struggles and share in your victories can provide a sense of validation and comfort. By offering a listening ear, words of encouragement, or a shoulder to lean on, fellow parents can create a safe space where feelings can be shared and relationships can be nurtured.

Lastly, building a support network of fellow parents can also create opportunities for personal growth and development. By engaging with others who have different perspectives and experiences, parents can learn new skills, broaden their horizons, and challenge their own beliefs and assumptions. The relationships formed within a support network can offer an opportunity for self-reflection and growth, as parents confront their own strengths and weaknesses, and learn from the successes and failures of others. By connecting with other parents, sharing experiences, and offering support, parents can create a community that can provide practical advice, emotional support, and opportunities for personal growth. Whether through parent groups, online forums, or community events, building a support network of fellow parents can help parents navigate the challenges and joys of raising children with confidence and resilience.

- Sharing parenting tips and resources

Parenting can be an incredibly rewarding yet challenging experience. As parents, we all want what is best for our children and strive to provide them with the love, support, and guidance they need to thrive. However, navigating the world of parenting can sometimes feel overwhelming, especially with the constant stream of conflicting information and advice available from various sources. This is where sharing parenting tips and resources can be incredibly beneficial. By sharing our own experiences and the strategies that have worked for us, we can help each other navigate the ups and downs of parenthood and create a supportive community of like-minded individuals who are all working towards the same goal of raising happy and healthy children.

When it comes to sharing parenting tips and resources, it is important to keep in mind that every child is unique and what works for one may not necessarily work for another. However, there are some universal principles that can help guide us in our parenting journey. Communication is key when it comes to parenting, both with our children and with other parents. By fostering open and honest communication with our children, we can better understand their needs and concerns and create a safe and nurturing environment for them to grow and learn. Similarly, by sharing our own experiences and strategies with other parents, we can learn from each other and gain new insights and perspectives that can help us become better parents.

One of the most valuable parenting tips that I have learned is the importance of setting boundaries and establishing routines. Children thrive on routine and structure, as it provides them with a sense of security and predictability. Setting boundaries and enforcing rules helps children learn about responsibility and consequences, while also helping them develop important skills such as self-discipline and time management. By setting clear expectations and sticking to them consistently, we can create a harmonious and peaceful home environment where both parents and children feel respected and valued.

Another important parenting tip is the power of positive reinforcement. Children respond much better to praise and encouragement than they do to criticism and punishment. By acknowledging and rewarding good behavior, we can help reinforce positive habits and values in our children. This not only boosts their self-esteem and confidence but also strengthens our bond with them. Taking the time to praise our children for their efforts and achievements, no matter how small, can go a long way in building a positive and supportive relationship based on mutual respect and appreciation.

In addition to setting boundaries and using positive reinforcement, it is also important to practice active listening as a parent. Listening to our children with an open mind and empathetic heart can help us better understand their thoughts, feelings, and needs. It is easy to fall into the trap of assuming that we know what is best for our children, but by actively listening to them, we can gain valuable insights into their perspective and build a stronger connection with them. By validating their emotions and showing genuine interest in what they have to say, we can create a safe space for our children to communicate openly and honestly with us.

Furthermore, seeking out and sharing parenting resources can be incredibly helpful in navigating the challenges of parenthood. From books and articles to online forums and support groups, there are a wealth of resources available to parents that can provide valuable information and guidance on a wide range of parenting topics. By staying informed and seeking out new ideas and perspectives, we can continue to grow and evolve as parents and become more effective in raising our children. Sharing these resources with other parents can also help create a sense of community and support, as we can learn from each other's experiences and help each other through the ups and downs of parenting. By sharing our own experiences and strategies, we can help each other navigate the challenges of parenthood and create a supportive community where we can learn from each other and grow together. By keeping an open mind, practicing active listening, and seeking out valuable resources, we can become better parents and raise confident, resilient, and well-adjusted children. Remember, we are all in this together, and by supporting each other, we can create a brighter future for our children.

Chapter 15: Balancing Work and Family Life

- Strategies for managing a successful career and family responsibilities

Managing a successful career while also tending to family responsibilities can be a challenging balancing act for many individuals. In today's fast-paced world, the demands of work and family can often seem overwhelming and it can be difficult to navigate the competing priorities. However, with the right strategies and mindset, it is possible to effectively manage both areas of your life and thrive in both your professional and personal roles. In this article, we will explore some key strategies for successfully juggling career and family responsibilities, including time management, setting boundaries, seeking support, and practicing self-care.

One of the most critical strategies for managing a successful career and family responsibilities is effective time management. With limited hours in the day, it is essential to prioritize tasks and allocate your time wisely between work and family commitments. Creating a schedule or to-do list can help you stay organized and ensure that you are meeting your deadlines and responsibilities in both areas of your life. Additionally, it is important to be realistic about what you can accomplish in a given day and learn to say no to additional obligations that may interfere with your ability to balance work and family effectively.

Setting boundaries is another crucial aspect of successfully managing career and family responsibilities. It is essential to establish clear boundaries between work and home life to prevent burnout and maintain a healthy work-life balance. This may involve setting limits on work hours, unplugging from technology during family time, or establishing boundaries with colleagues and supervisors about your availability outside of work hours. By setting boundaries, you can create a sense of structure and predictability in your life, which can help reduce stress and improve your overall well-being.

Seeking support from others is also an important strategy for managing a successful career and family responsibilities. It is essential to build a strong support network of friends, family, and colleagues who can offer assistance, guidance, and encouragement when needed. Whether it is asking for help with childcare, delegating tasks at work, or simply venting to a trusted confidante, having a support system in place can make the task of balancing career and family responsibilities feel less isolating and overwhelming. Additionally, seeking out professional resources, such as career coaches or family therapists, can provide valuable tools and strategies for managing the competing demands of work and family.

Practicing self-care is another key strategy for successfully managing a career and family responsibilities. It is essential to prioritize your physical and emotional well-being in order to maintain the energy and focus needed to excel in both areas of your life. This may involve making time for exercise, getting enough sleep, eating well, and engaging in activities that bring you joy and relaxation. Additionally, practicing mindfulness techniques, such as meditation or deep breathing exercises, can help reduce stress and improve your ability to handle the challenges of balancing work and family responsibilities. However, with the right strategies and mindset, it is possible to effectively juggle both areas of your life and thrive in your professional and personal roles. By utilizing strategies such as effective time management, setting boundaries, seeking support, and practicing self-care, you can create a sense of balance and fulfillment in your life while excelling in both your career and family responsibilities. Remember that it is okay to ask for help when needed and to prioritize your well-being in order to achieve success and happiness in all areas of your life.

- Finding time for self-care and relaxation

In today's fast-paced and demanding world, finding time for self-care and relaxation has become more important than ever. With the constant pressure to excel in our careers, maintain meaningful relationships, and juggle numerous responsibilities, it can be easy to neglect our own well-being. However, self-care is essential for our physical, mental, and emotional health. It allows us to recharge our batteries, reduce stress, and improve our overall quality of life.

One of the biggest challenges in finding time for self-care and relaxation is the perception that it is a luxury rather than a necessity. Many people believe that they simply do not have the time to prioritize self-care in their busy schedules. However, the truth is that self-care should be viewed as an essential part of a healthy lifestyle, rather than an indulgence. By taking care of ourselves, we are better equipped to handle the challenges and demands of daily life.

In order to find time for self-care and relaxation, it is important to prioritize and schedule it into our daily routine. This may require setting boundaries with work and other commitments, and learning to say no to activities that do not align with our self-care goals. It can also involve delegating tasks to others, or seeking support from friends and family members. By making self-care a priority and carving out dedicated time for it, we can ensure that we are taking care of ourselves in a consistent and sustainable way.

Another key aspect of finding time for self-care and relaxation is understanding what activities and practices are most beneficial for our individual needs. Self-care can look different for everyone, and it is important to explore a variety of activities to find what works best for you. This may include activities such as exercise, meditation, journaling, spending time in nature, or engaging in hobbies and interests that bring you joy. By experimenting with different self-care practices, you can discover what helps you to feel rejuvenated and balanced.

In addition to scheduling time for self-care, it is also important to create a supportive environment that encourages relaxation and well-being. This may involve setting up a designated self-care space in your home, where you can retreat and unwind. It may also require setting boundaries with technology and creating time for digital detoxes. By creating a physical and mental space that is conducive to relaxation, you can better prioritize your self-care and make it a regular part of your routine.

Finding time for self-care and relaxation can also involve developing a positive mindset and self-care routine. This may include practicing gratitude, self-compassion, and mindfulness on a daily basis. By cultivating a positive outlook and taking care of our emotional well-being, we can better manage stress and anxiety, and improve our overall mental health. Developing a self-care routine that incorporates these practices can help us to feel more grounded, peaceful, and resilient in the face of life's challenges. By prioritizing self-care, scheduling time for relaxation, and creating a supportive environment for well-being, we can ensure that we are taking care of ourselves in a consistent and sustainable way. By exploring different self-care practices and developing a positive mindset, we can better manage stress, improve our mental health, and enhance our quality of life. Making self-care a priority is not only beneficial for ourselves, but also for those around us, as we are better equipped to show up as our best selves in all aspects of our lives.

Chapter 16: Navigating Transitions and Milestones

- Helping your child adjust to changes like moving, starting school, or adolescence

Helping your child adjust to changes can be a challenging and emotional process for both the child and the parent. Whether it's moving to a new location, starting a new school, or experiencing the changes of adolescence, it's important to provide support and guidance to help make the transition as smooth as possible. Change can be intimidating for children, as they may feel uncertain or anxious about what lies ahead. By offering reassurance, understanding, and encouragement, you can help your child navigate through these changes with confidence and resilience.

When moving to a new location, children may experience a range of emotions such as sadness, fear, or excitement. It's important to acknowledge their feelings and validate their emotions, as this will help them feel heard and understood. Encourage open communication with your child and allow them to express their concerns or worries about the move. By listening attentively and offering reassurance, you can help your child feel supported during this transition. Additionally, involving your child in the moving process can help them feel more in control and empowered. Allow them to pack their belongings, say goodbye to their old home, and explore their new surroundings. This sense of involvement can help your child adjust more easily to the change.

Starting a new school can be a daunting experience for children, as they are faced with unfamiliar surroundings, new peers, and different academic expectations. It's important to prepare your child for this transition by discussing what to expect and offering practical tips for navigating the new school environment. Encourage your child to get involved in extracurricular activities, join clubs, or make new friends, as this can help them feel more connected and engaged in their new school community. Additionally, establish open lines of communication with your child's teachers and school staff to address any concerns or challenges that may arise. By working together as a team, you can support your child's academic and social success during this transition period.

Adolescence is a time of significant change and development for children, as they undergo physical, emotional, and social transformations. It's normal for adolescents to experience mood swings, identity exploration, and conflicts with authority figures during this period. As a parent, it's important to offer understanding and flexibility as your child navigates through the challenges of adolescence. Maintain an open and supportive relationship with your child, and be available to listen and provide guidance when needed. Encourage your child to express their thoughts and feelings in a healthy and constructive manner, and offer a non-judgmental space for them to explore their evolving identity. By fostering a sense of trust and communication, you can help your child navigate through the changes of adolescence with confidence and self-awareness. By providing support, reassurance, and guidance, you can help your child navigate through these transitions with resilience and confidence. Encourage open communication, involve your child in the process, and maintain a supportive relationship to help them feel empowered and connected during times of change. Remember that each child is unique, and may respond differently to change, so it's important to tailor your approach to meet your child's individual needs. Together, you and your child can work through transitions and challenges with strength and positivity, fostering a sense of resilience and adaptability that will serve them well in the future.

- Celebrating achievements and milestones together

Celebrating achievements and milestones together is an important aspect of fostering a positive and supportive work environment. Acknowledging and recognizing the hard work and dedication that individuals put into their personal and professional goals not only boosts morale but also encourages continued success. Whether it's a team hitting a sales target, an individual receiving a promotion, or a department reaching a significant milestone, these accomplishments should be celebrated and shared with the entire organization.

By celebrating achievements and milestones together, organizations can create a sense of unity and camaraderie among employees. When individuals feel valued and appreciated for their contributions, they are more likely to be engaged and motivated to excel in their roles. This can lead to higher levels of job satisfaction, improved performance, and increased productivity. Recognizing and celebrating successes also helps to build a positive company culture where employees feel supported and encouraged to reach their full potential.

In addition to boosting morale and fostering a positive work environment, celebrating achievements and milestones together can also help to promote a sense of teamwork and collaboration. When individuals are recognized for their accomplishments, it not only validates their hard work but also demonstrates the importance of working together towards a common goal. By celebrating as a team, employees are able to see the impact of their collective efforts and how collaboration can lead to success. This can strengthen relationships among team members and encourage continued collaboration in the future.

Furthermore, celebrating achievements and milestones together can serve as a learning opportunity for both individuals and the organization as a whole. By reflecting on the steps that led to success and sharing best practices with others, employees can learn from each other's experiences and apply those lessons to future projects. This knowledge-sharing can help to drive innovation and continuous improvement within the organization. Additionally, celebrating achievements can inspire others to set and pursue their own goals, creating a culture of ambition and growth.

There are many ways that organizations can celebrate achievements and milestones together. This can range from simple gestures such as offering congratulations and thank yous to more formal recognition programs and events. Some organizations choose to hold regular team meetings where achievements are highlighted and celebrated, while others may opt for annual awards ceremonies or team-building activities to recognize outstanding accomplishments. Regardless of the format, the key is to ensure that recognition is sincere, timely, and tailored to the individual or team being celebrated. By recognizing and acknowledging the hard work and dedication of employees, organizations can boost morale, promote teamwork, and foster a culture of continuous improvement. Through celebrations and recognition, employees are motivated to excel in their roles, collaborate with their colleagues, and drive innovation within the organization. By prioritizing the celebration of achievements, organizations can create a culture of success that benefits both individuals and the organization as a whole.

Chapter 17: Conclusion

- Reflecting on your parenting journey

The journey of parenthood is a unique and multifaceted experience that can be both challenging and rewarding. Reflecting on one's parenting journey can provide valuable insights into the successes and struggles that have shaped the growth and development of both parents and children. In this reflective process, parents can gain a deeper understanding of their parenting style, beliefs, and values, as well as identify areas for growth and improvement.

One of the key aspects of reflecting on the parenting journey is recognizing the importance of self-awareness and emotional intelligence. Parents who are able to understand their own emotions, triggers, and reactions are better equipped to respond to their children in a mindful and compassionate manner. By being aware of their own strengths and weaknesses, parents can cultivate a positive and nurturing environment that fosters healthy growth and development in their children.

Another important aspect of reflecting on the parenting journey is acknowledging the impact of one's own upbringing and childhood experiences. Many parents unconsciously repeat patterns of behavior and communication that they learned from their own parents, which can influence their relationship with their children. By reflecting on these patterns and making a conscious effort to break negative cycles, parents can create a more positive and supportive home environment for their children.

Furthermore, reflecting on the parenting journey involves examining the values and beliefs that shape one's approach to parenting. Parents may hold different beliefs about discipline, education, and family dynamics, which can influence their parenting decisions and interactions with their children. By reflecting on these beliefs and considering their impact on their children, parents can make informed choices that align with their values and promote the well-being of their family.

In addition to self-awareness and values, reflecting on the parenting journey also involves recognizing the importance of establishing clear and consistent boundaries with children. Setting boundaries helps children understand expectations and learn self-discipline, while also promoting a sense of security and stability within the family. By reflecting on their own boundaries and communication style, parents can create a harmonious and respectful relationship with their children that fosters mutual trust and understanding.

Moreover, reflecting on the parenting journey requires parents to be open to feedback and willing to adapt their parenting approach as their children grow and change. Children are constantly evolving and developing, and their needs and challenges may shift over time. By reflecting on their parenting journey and being open to new ideas and perspectives, parents can continue to support and guide their children in a positive and effective way. By cultivating self-awareness, examining values and beliefs, setting boundaries, and staying open to feedback, parents can navigate the challenges of parenthood with wisdom and compassion. Through reflection and self-improvement, parents can create a nurturing and supportive environment that fosters the growth and well-being of their children.

- Committing to continued growth and learning as a parent

Committing to continued growth and learning as a parent is a crucial aspect of raising children in today's complex and ever-changing world. As parents, we are faced with the responsibility of nurturing and guiding our children through the various stages of their development, from infancy to adulthood. In order to effectively fulfill this role, it is important for parents to recognize that parenting is a continuous learning process that requires ongoing growth and education.

One of the key elements of committing to continued growth and learning as a parent is the willingness to adapt and evolve in response to the changing needs and challenges of our children. As our children grow and develop, so too must our parenting strategies and approaches. What works for one child may not work for another, and what is effective in one situation may not be as successful in another. By remaining open to new ideas and approaches, parents can better meet the unique needs of their children and help them thrive in today's complex society.

Another important aspect of committing to continued growth and learning as a parent is seeking out opportunities for education and self-improvement. This can include attending parenting workshops, reading books and articles on child development, and seeking guidance from experts in the field of child psychology. By investing time and effort into expanding our knowledge and skills as parents, we can better equip ourselves to meet the challenges of raising children in today's fast-paced and ever-changing world.

Additionally, committing to continued growth and learning as a parent involves being willing to reflect on our own parenting practices and seek feedback from others. It can be helpful to engage in self-reflection and evaluate our strengths and weaknesses as parents. By being open to constructive criticism and feedback from others, we can identify areas where we can improve and make necessary changes to our parenting approach.

Moreover, committing to continued growth and learning as a parent also involves fostering a growth mindset in our children. By instilling a love of learning and a willingness to embrace new challenges in our children, we can help them develop the skills and resilience needed to navigate the complexities of the modern world. Encouraging our children to seek out new experiences, learn from their mistakes, and persevere in the face of obstacles can help them develop the confidence and fortitude needed to succeed in life. By remaining open to new ideas and approaches, seeking out opportunities for education and self-improvement, reflecting on our own parenting practices, and fostering a growth mindset in our children, we can better equip ourselves to meet the challenges of raising children in the 21st century. Ultimately, by committing to continued growth and learning as parents, we can better support our children in their development and help them reach their full potential.